This book belongs to:

FOREVER

LOVE ME
chocolate
BE MINE

LOVES ME
NOT!

YOU ARE DEAD TO ME!

LovE SucKS

LOVE
ETERNAL

I Love myself

LOVE is SWEET

BROKEN

LOVE
BE MINE!

WAITING ON Love
TILL DEATH

TRUE LOVE
chocolate

RIP
FOREVER

BE MINE
FOREVER
LOVE

LOVE

LOVE
BE MINE

Love

XOX

Thank you for purchasing this coloring book, one of many in the Chubby Mermaid series. Please don't forget to sign into Amzon.com – Deborah Muller Coloring Books and leave a review.

Follow me on Facebook
Chubby Mermaid Art by Deborah Muller

Join my Coloring Group on Facebook
Deborah Muller's Coloring Group

Instagram
Chubby Mermaid Art

Etsy
Chubby Mermaid

Pinterest
Deborah Muller Chubby Mermaid Art

Email
Chubbymermaid@hotmail.com

Website
ChubbyMermaidArt.com

Made in the USA
Las Vegas, NV
05 May 2024

89575446R00044